AUDITION
SECRETS
Vol. I

AUDITION SECRETS
Vol. I

The Behind The Scenes Guidebook For Nailing
More Auditions And Booking More Jobs

Justin Bell Guarini

Published by

CHECKMATE PRESS
checkmatepress.com

Published by Checkmate Press / McLean Media Group, LLC
4364 Glenwood Dr
Bozeman, MT 59718
www.checkmatepress.com

Audition Secrets Vol. 1/ Justin Bell Guarini. -- 1st ed.
ISBN 978-1-7321781-1-3

The Publisher has strived to be as accurate and complete as possible in the creation of this book.

This book is not intended for use as a source of legal, business, accounting or financial advice. All readers are advised to seek services of competent professionals in legal, business, accounting, and finance fields.

In practical advice books, like anything else in life, there are no guarantees of income or results made. Readers are cautioned to rely on their own judgment about their individual circumstances and act accordingly.

While all attempts have been made to verify information provided in this publication, the Publisher assumes no responsibility for errors, omissions, or contrary interpretation of the subject matter herein. Any perceived slights of specific persons, peoples, or organizations are unintentional.

This book is brought to you by:

The Warrior Artist Alliance

And

Justin Bell Guarini

TABLE OF CONTENTS

PREFACE

"I could have done so much better."

Have you ever walked out of an audition room and had that thought?

I have, about a thousand times...leaving the audition room, exiting the stage, after the last note of a song, in the rehearsal room and even after a class.

I've felt that way more times than I could ever count... but feeling that way is "normal", right?

Wrong.

For decades, I went through "The Cycle":
- Trying to find the right agent.
- Trying to get audition appointments.
- Working as hard as I could to learn the songs and scenes.
- Trying to beat lyrics and lines into my head.
- Making sure I looked perfect by putting together a million different outfits and/or wasting money on new clothes.
- Trying to juggle 'real life' with my auditions.
- Feeling good about myself, and my chances, at first.
- Feeling more and more nervous as the audition day approached.

- Then feeling the confidence I had at home disintegrate once I got into the audition room.
- Walking out of the audition room reliving *every single mistake* I made and knowing I could have...should have...done so much better.
- Beating myself up for the rest of the week.
- Waiting to hear back from my agent.
- Worrying that my agent was going to lose faith in me because I wasn't booking jobs.
- Vowing to do better the next time.
- Spending more time and money on classes.

Then repeating the cycle over again from the top...again and again.

Can you relate to any of the parts of "The Cycle"?

Millions of us see this painful cycle as 'normal'...but is this really a normal way to live?

When you think about it...what we put ourselves through is completely insane...but millions of performers do it every day.

Millions of us just accept that this is what it takes in order to "make it" in this business.

Fuck that.

This book is an opening salvo in the war against what we consider "normal" in this business.

What most people outside of the entertainment and performance world don't understand is that what we artists do...moves humanity. The arts are vital to the health and stability of our cultures, our countries, and our entire world.

But we storytellers who open new doors, get doors slammed in our faces all the time. So why do we constantly come back for more?

One of the many reasons why is because we know that we are in the service of something bigger than ourselves. Because some piece of great art awoke something powerful inside us, and we want to use and share our gifts and that awakening with as many people as we can.

Because we know that there is something bigger at play...we take the rejection, the humiliation, and the slammed doors.

This book is one of the keys to a door that, when you walk through it, will completely revolutionize your career...and your life!

The old way of doing things has chained you to the same old results...

Audition. Despair. Repeat.

I want to show you how to break free from "The Cycle."

Just like you, I have experienced some success here and there, but mostly heartbreaking failures as I went around and around in "The Cycle."

Then one day after years and years of struggling...I finally achieved mind-blowing success on a national and international level.

In 2002, I went from being a kid who was grinding day in day and day out trying to get someone to just notice him in a business that was confusing in the best of times, to being a part of a huge television ratings juggernaut and beaming into over 30 million homes each week.

I went from having my Mom and Dad cheering me from the stands to having a legion of fans who made posters, tee-shirts, sent me gifts, voted hundreds of times for me each week, sang my songs, and even drove hundreds of miles to watch me perform live and meet me.

I went from bussing tables to a tour bus that took me around the country playing night after night to sold-out arenas with 30,000 screaming fans.

I lived in a huge compound in Bel Air with maid service. I was on the cover of magazines, newspapers, I was a guest host on "Live with Kelly Ripa," I booked a role on a new sitcom and was even interviewed by Oprah on The Oprah Winfrey Show...twice.

I was a star, and I had the world on a string.

I felt confident, powerful, and like I was finally living out my destiny. I was 22 and I had become a millionaire.

Then I had a big movie that was skewered in the press, and it tanked.

After that, I had an album that flopped.

I floundered.

Amidst all my personal and professional struggles, the entire world made a huge shift as social media came roaring in, reality TV exploded, and people's attention spans and patience got even shorter than before.

Almost as quickly as my star rose, it began to fade, and with it slowly...then more and more rapidly as I shrank away from the spotlight...so did my fans. Where once there were millions screaming my name, only a handful of devoted fan-friends remained.

Privately, I was bleeding money in the attempt to make it look to my peers like I was ok...still successful and "killing it." The old "fake it till you make it" model left me "faking it" more and more each day.

Eventually, things got so bad that I was barely treading water financially. I could see I was slowly drowning in debt.

What I couldn't see was my self-confidence evaporating as well. I didn't even realize it was completely gone until a girl I was dating told me how her sister said to her, "Your boyfriend is so funny and nice, but he's so deeply sad." At the time I laughed... and denied it.

...but in my heart, I knew she was right.

Publicly, I became the punch line to the jokes of late-night talk show hosts and only found out that I had been dropped from my record label because I was watching Tina Fey make a joke about it on Saturday Night Live's "Weekend Update."

Every day, for years, it felt like I was being blind-sided by some attack that ate away at everything I had built, and as I stood in the ashes of what was once a vibrant career and life...I made a choice.

In 2008, I chose to start over...and go back to my roots.

The Theater.

INTRODUCTION:
THE THREE DOORS

There's a difference between fear and paralysis. And I've learned that I don't have to "grow up" to be open to opportunity, to be willing to step through doors without being pushed.

I just have to be brave.

I just have to be slightly braver than I am scared.

- Victoria Schwab, author

Before I begin, let me share my intentions for you as you read this book:

1. I am going to give you a quick and previously unpublished glimpse into my history and backstory, so you can understand why I'm inviting you to learn about a better way to work and live!

2. I am going to introduce you to some fresh ideas, challenge your long-held beliefs, and show you a new way of seeing the roles we can play in reshaping this industry.

3. Finally, I am going to give you what the title of this book promises: five easy to learn and powerful Audition Secrets that you can use right away to take your auditions and performances to the next level.

I believe it is possible to nail every audition, every time.

I believe it is possible to nail every performance, every time.

This book is just the beginning of the journey, and I want to be your guide as we explore the promise of and the path to achieving your unique version of success and deep satisfaction.

5,6,7,8...let's go!

~

One of the greatest memories in my career was when I was 15, and I stepped onto the stage for the first time at "Capers! Dinner Theater" in Pipersville, Pennsylvania.

Set 30 feet back from a two-lane highway that led North into the farmlands that we locals lovingly call "Pennsyl-tucky," the Pied Piper Restaurant looked to passersby like a run-of-the-mill establishment with a mural of a cat dressed as the Pied Piper painted on it. A ribbon of music notes guided your eye and a few unlucky painted mice to the front door.

Inside was where the magic began. Attached to the restaurant was a completely refurbished dinner theater. Everything was 1995-sparkling-new (think wood-paneling and a lot of brass). Everything that is, except for the stage.

Chipped, from Lord knows how many tap routines, and painted black to cover the many dings, the stage was a stubby-legged rectangle just big enough to fit on it five or six huddled actors (find a window!) and three white doors.

Set in a large rectangular frame, the doors were identical and connected, so that there was a door on the left, one in the center, and one on the right.

Three doors that served as slightly wobbly entrances, exits, scene shifts, and the only structures we could hide behind to change and exchange costumes and wigs.

Looking back on it now, the setup was about as basic as it gets...but at the time it was like the Palace Theater to me...and I loved the thrill of every moment onstage.

It was where, for the first time, I heard the magic of Schwartz and actually had a place outside of my bedroom to sing Sondheim! It was where I fell in love with the process, the work, and the intense passion that is the foundation of American Theater.

Fourteen years later (at age 29), and 3,000 miles away from the memory of that dinner theater's first kiss I stood and stared at those three doors again. They sat before me, as rickety as ever...but this time, they were on the stage of my mind.

I thought back to how I took a chance on a TV show no one had ever heard of called "American Idol," and I related it to making the choice to go into the door on the *Left*... I had no idea where this door would lead.

Well, what a ride it was!!

I walked back out of *that* door tired, careworn (album flop, movie flop, working to the point of exhaustion, and rotting in the wasteland of Hollywood culture) and with what my Southern-born father likes to say: "More problems than you can shake a stick at,"...but I was still alive. I had made it out, and a truly creative spirit never rests, right?

So, as I gathered myself to try again to make my mark on the world, I thought that my path must reside beyond the imaginary *Center Door*. But when I tried to open it, I found it was locked...I even tried looking through the keyhole, but all I could see was darkness. Frustrated by yet another setback, I couldn't understand at the time why it was locked.

Years later, I'd learn how life's greatest treasures often come to us when we're ready for them, not when we want them.

Having only one option left, I tried the third imaginary door, the door to the *Right*, and it was open! To my surprise and delight, I found the potential for a new life and career waiting for me on the other side.

Broadway...the apex of the theatrical world!

Out of the ashes of one childhood dream, like a Phoenix, sprang the realization that I could pursue another childhood dream that had been patiently waiting for me in the wings.

I had hope again, and I was brought back to a "fork in the road" moment where I made a decision that forever changed my life in 2002.

~

While I was in college, majoring in Vocal Performance and Musical Theater, I auditioned for "The Lion King" on Broadway. I got a few callbacks and based on the success of my auditions got invited to be a part of a master class that served as a training ground for booking the show.

The casting team and producers loved everything I did, and they wanted me for the show, but the "timing wasn't right". So, they told me to wait, and I waited...for 3 years!

I didn't have an agent, so I had no one to follow up for me, and the Company Manager would call me once a year or so and ask me to come in and meet...but it never led to anything.

Then towards the end of this 3-year dance came "American Idol"...and wouldn't you know it...the week I was going to fly out to Hollywood for "Hollywood Week " the casting director for "The Lion King" called me and said, "We want you, and we finally have a place for you in the show. When can you start?"

Fork. In. The. Road.

I had spent the better part of five years dreaming of my Broadway debut, auditioning, working an awesome survival job, and waiting for "the call"...and just as I was going to get my prize...I had booked another gig and was set to jet to the West Coast for a gig that I could be potentially cut from the day after I landed.

I was confused, and scared, but I immediately knew what to do. Compromise! I asked the casting director if I could get back to him in one week with an answer. I knew that by the time seven days had passed I'd either have booked the full gig in LA or be back home and available to make my debut.

Seven days passed, and my deadline had arrived. I had calculated incorrectly and I didn't know whether or not I would actually make the top 30 of the singing competition yet...but I'll never forget the memory of being in the theater of the Pasadena Civic Center where we were taping Hollywood Week, looking at the stage, walking down the aisle and unexpectedly bursting into tears.

True story, I'm not taking poetic license here. I'm not an easy crier, so the experience was extra strange for me. As I tried to hide my tears from the people around me, I felt a ping in my heart that said "this is right" ...and in that moment I knew what I had to do.

I called the Casting Director and told them how honored I was and what a dream come true being in "The Lion King" would be, but that I had another opportunity I was going to pursue because it felt right in my heart.

That one decision would take me on an amazing and mind-blowing seven-year journey around the world and back again...and when I landed bruised and much the worse for wear, I was thankful just to have made it out alive.

~

I had come full circle, back that fateful fork in the road. Now I had the opportunity to take the other path and revisit my roots in the Theater. So, I began to dust off my passion for the process, and just as easily as some folks fall again for an old lover they haven't seen in years but randomly bump into on the train, I slipped right back into...

"The Cycle."

I went back to my roots, started over, and paid my dues just like everyone else. I went on audition after audition...but this time I showed up with the stigma of my public failures. Now I was seen by the people on the other side of the table through the lens of "Who's this reality tv guy trying to be on Broadway?" Now, I was trying to make it all over again while bearing the full weight of the private pain I hid a way from everyone...the pain and confusion that came from the trauma of going through the soaring highs and fathomless lows of the Hollywood meat grinder.

Again, I failed, I floundered, and I learned the hard way until I booked my first Broadway show, *Women On The Verge Of A Nervous Breakdown*, where Tony winners Patti LuPone and Brian Stokes Mitchell played my Mother and Father.

I set out on an outstanding Broadway journey in the theater district of Manhattan that would lead me to:

- Play alongside Billie Joe Armstrong in Green Day's *American Idiot*
- Join the "Brotherhood of The Tight White Pants" as "Fiyero" in *Wicked*
- Play "Paris" in my most beloved literary work *Romeo + Juliet*
- Star in *Encores!* beautiful revival of *Paint Your Wagon*
- and work alongside of some of my most beloved peers in Broadway's first all A Cappella musical *In Transit*.

So why, at the end of the day, did I feel so empty?

I was DOING IT! I had what so many people in our business covet: consistent work at one of the highest levels of the Entertainment Business. I was making money, I had fans, I had like-minded colleagues and friends, I had thousands of hours of treading the boards on the Great White Way under my belt...I was in NEW YORK, BABY!!

...but it wasn't enough.

I realized that I still felt that *I* wasn't enough.

Even though I had success and was well-regarded among my peers and employers...I came to the shocking realization that once again I had entered...

"The Cycle."

I didn't break free from it because I was booking jobs...I just leveled up in the same game!

I entered a whole new cycle... but this time, the pressure and the stakes were much higher, and I was not only responsible for my own shortcomings, but I was jockeying for the best position and trying to shine in a much smaller and tighter crowd of extremely shiny people...

** You may wonder why I'm complaining. These are good problems to have, right? This is the stuff you face when you've hit the "big time"...but at the end of the day, a problem is a problem, and when you live under the constant and ever-increasing pressure for long enough without solid foundation to fall back on, you begin to bend...then eventually break like so many people in our business have**

Once again, I had entered "The Cycle" (Level 2):

- Having more than one agent send you opportunity after opportunity each day and having to choose which ones to take and not take...but being scared to let any of them pass by just in case it's "the one" or you by turning down work you somehow lose your mojo.

- Being called directly into the final round of auditions for projects where the whole creative team and producers are expecting your first try to blow them away.

- Having to "re-train" directors/producers to see you in a different light because of the kind of typecasting success can bring.

- Booking a great job, creating a close bond with and connection to your castmates...a *family*, and then once the project is over, breaking apart and promising you'll keep in touch, but drifting away day by day.

- Having to worry during a show about who is in the audience, and, when you know there's an important Producer/Director/Casting Director/Critic present, trying to put on a show that ISN'T self-conscious.

- Juggling your constant need to be looking ahead to the next paycheck, or job with the needs and demands of your Lover/Spouse/Partner/Kids/Pets.

- Worrying that you'll have enough weeks to cover your health insurance.

- Being treated like the "Hired Help" by powerful players in the business.

- Being ultra-careful not to say anything in interviews that could be taken out of context and held against you.

- Doing tons of free promotion that lines other people's pockets but gives you very little return on your own investment of time and money.

- Getting injured or sick and having to miss shows and paychecks. *Still* worrying that your agent is going to lose faith in you because you aren't booking enough high-level jobs.

- *Still* walking out of the audition room re-living every single mistake you made and knowing you could have...should have...done so much better. That now you're expected to be "flawless" and anything less equates to "failure"

This is by no means the whole list...and it varies from performer to performer, but do you see anything here you can relate to?

I lived all of this and more every day I set foot out my door and went to work on my craft.

I felt empty but beat myself up for being ungrateful for the success I had.

I thought that this was just the way it was supposed to be...the "price of success."

I wondered if there was something more...or a better way to go about my process. But between my work, my family, and the commitments I was making to others, I didn't have time to figure it all out.

I kept going, kept spinning around and around in "The Cycle." ...until one of the biggest Broadway auditions of my life came around.

~

This show was, and still is, HUGE...and I was being asked to audition as a replacement for two different roles that are, for me, both roles of a lifetime.

I love this show, I will forever love the team of people that created it, and because of that, I was determined to book it.

I learned and memorized 20 songs, auditioned for the creative team/producers six times over a period of three months.

I worked harder than I ever have before on being the very best I could be, taking care of my voice and body like never before, taking each note that the creative team gave me and burning them into my performance so that I could be even better the next time I came into the room.

I even contacted the person who was in the role(s) at the time and asked him in-depth questions about the character to help me create a performance that was as compelling as his was.

I broke down the script and lyrics and studied them moment by moment trying to mine every last bit of truth and nuance out of them.

I studied performances that I could find online that mirrored the role I was going for. I was doing *everything* it took to make my vision a reality.

Then the time came for the creative team to choose which role I was going to get. After months of toil on my part, after asking me to come in repeatedly and give everything I had and pushing me to give more...

They didn't give me either role.

They just said "no."

I was baffled. My agents were baffled. Even the Casting Director was baffled.

Rejection I can handle. It's a daily part of what we do isn't it? What I couldn't stomach was the fact that I didn't even get the courtesy of a reason why they said "no." They made me jump through the audition equivalent of flaming hoops while wearing a tutu...the least they could have done was give me some feedback. At least I could have some closure...something to fix for the future, some peace of mind.

I was crushed.

I had done everything right...more right than I'd ever done it before...and it still wasn't enough. I felt angry, and I felt like I'd been strung along. For nothing.

After a decade of giving my all at the Broadway level to climb higher and higher on the ladder, my spirit ended up being crushed right before I got a role that would actually make people stand up and notice all I'd done.

Once again, I was faced with a choice...and decided to take a break from the pain and step back.

I made the choice to get out of "The Cycle" and reevaluate if I even wanted to keep going in what felt more and more like a rat race.

A race where the wealthy and powerful looked down on us as we entertained them by scurrying around and around in a maze, searching for the small bits of cheese they would drop in hidden corners just to entice us to keep playing their game.

~

Frustrated and alone, I found myself once again staring at The Three Doors in my mind.

This time, I tried the Center Door again...and *again* it was locked.

I didn't know which way to turn.

So, with nowhere else to go, I turned inward and began to ask myself questions like:

"What can I do that hasn't already been tried to break 'The Cycle' of pain, humiliation, and disorientation that this business causes me?"

"Why do some people who aren't any smarter or more talented, or hardworking than I am, seem to go so far while I still struggle to even get off the ground some days?"

"How can I stop chasing this vague image of success in my head that I call "Making It" and start creating my own destiny and my own "luck" on a consistent basis?"

"How can I feel more fulfilled?"

Questions like those lit a fire in me that grew and grew and burns so fiercely that it has inspired me to invite you into this journey with me.

The trials, the mystery, the confusion, and the "injustice" ignited in me an obsession with the process of auditioning and with what it was like to see the audition from both sides of the table.

I studied and interviewed some of the biggest Casting Directors in our business. I asked in-depth questions of my mentors, the theater and entertainment superstars that I was friends with, and my peers who work their tails off every day about how they approached the work, their processes before they even got on the stage, and how they dealt with "The Cycle."

I studied the work of the one-name performers and luminaries in our business and broke down what they were doing with their bodies, faces and voices...and then applied what they did to my own work on stage and television.

I trained my body to increase my endurance and focused my mind with meditation and breath work so that I could to bring to bear the fullness of my skill sets and depth of my emotions in auditions and performances.

I trained like a Warrior...and then during a meditation, the phrase "Warrior Artist" floated into my mind...

"Warrior Artist"

That is what I wanted to be, and that is what I've become.

If you are reading this book and have gotten this far, I believe that you are (or are in the process of becoming) one of the Warrior Artists that get up each day, put on their armor, and go to battle against the ridiculous odds that we face in this business.

I know it sounds a bit dramatic...but have you ever tried to explain to someone outside of our world about what a typical day in the life is like for us...the stress, the daily humiliation, the highs and lows, the petty dramas we have to deal with, and the massive amount of information we have to take in and execute perfectly at almost a moment's notice?

That's just scratching the surface of what we deal with every day.

Seeing things through that lens, calling ourselves Warrior Artists and speaking in terms of the "armor" we wear to survive each day doesn't sound so dramatic, does it?

To serve my fellow Warrior Artists, I created The Warrior Artist Podcast with a ton of episodes designed just for you.

I used what I'd learned and the momentum I'd generated to create more success in my work, and I booked more jobs with greater ease, but I still didn't feel the deep sense of reward I was looking for...until a friend asked me if I could help her daughter out with an audition.

I applied what I had learned to help another performer out, and through the process of helping that young lady (and others like her) work through the material, I fell in love with teaching.

I knew I could never give up performing, but now another world filled with new possibilities opened up to me. I found that the more I taught, the more I grew as a performer and a person.

I took on more private clients and refined what I was teaching them so that the process was fun, easy to learn, easy to apply, and made for more powerful and more fully connected performances.

Finally, I took all of my experience at the highest levels of the entertainment business, all that I had learned from my mentors, industry leaders, and peers, and every piece of wisdom I had gathered, and I decided to share it with the people who could benefit from it the most...

My people.

My Theater People.

My fellow Warrior Artists.

When I made the decision to serve as many as I could instead of just myself, the Center Door in my mind that had remained so stubbornly closed... unlocked, and I stepped into a world where I didn't feel alone anymore.

I decided to create a book called Audition Secrets based on some of the lessons I'd learned and strategies I'd used and seen other performers use.

I decided to create a community where other Warrior Artists and I could tell our stories and be ourselves without shame, judgment, or fear of retribution.

A community where I could share all my experience and wisdom so that others on the path could avoid the pitfalls that snagged me.

A community where I could bring in the very best teachers, mentors, stars, and thought leaders to share their high-level knowledge and wisdom so that anyone anywhere in the world could receive the best training our world has to offer.

I hired a team of people to help me create and maintain a community where I could share the

Warrior Artist & Audition Secrets message with thousands of like-minded artists and interact with them one-on-one and in groups.

Together we share our stories.

Together we share our victories and help each other through our defeats.

Together we take the power back from the people who have fooled us into thinking that we are powerless.

Together we help each other push through our "Center Doors" and step into the highest paths we are meant to take.

Together. We. Rise.

~

If you're interested in learning more and discovering the clarity, passion, and power that being a part of a like-minded community can bring you, then I invite you to join our free Audition Secrets Facebook group by going to:

www.facebook.com/groups/auditionsecretsvip/

(If you haven't already joined.)

Come and join other passionate, powerful, and purpose-driven artists that you can learn from, grow with, and you'll find a place where we can all RISE TOGETHER.

INTRODUCTION: AUTHOR'S NOTE

Before I get to the Audition Secrets, I want to set you up for success. You will get the maximum benefit out of this book if you are:

- *Open* and *willing* to learn something new.
- *Brave* enough to test the ideas and concepts out for yourself in the audition room and on the stage.
- *Ready* to play full out.

You have in your hands an opportunity to begin the shift toward the success, confidence, and clarity you deserve to feel every single time you walk into an audition room or onto a stage

If you apply the principles and methods I'm about to share with you, you will begin to separate yourself from the thousands of other actors around you.

This book is just the beginning of a whole new way to approach your next audition or performance.

This book is the first of many good tools I'm going to give you to walk into an audition room and own it.

You deserve to share your gift with your community and the world. You absolutely deserve to have the career and success you've worked so hard to prepare for. It is my honor and privilege to do all I can to help you achieve success.

Enjoy "Audition Secrets" and welcome to The Warrior Artist Alliance.

~ Justin Bell Guarini

CHAPTER 1:
OWN EVERY
SINGLE MISTAKE

Never say, 'oops!'
Always say,
'Ahh, interesting.'

- Anonymous

As performers, we spend decades learning how to speak and sing *words*. How to move our bodies in time to the rhythms and sounds we hear. How to give of ourselves and our gifts so deeply and freely that through the simple act of being present we can literally infuse the air around us with the electricity of our spirit.

From a very young age, we quickly come to understand, from the joyous gales of laughter they can bring us or the bitter tears of anguish they can draw from us, that *words have power*.

With that in mind, there are two words you should never, ever, ever, ever "say" in an audition room or on a stage. Those words?

"I'm sorry."

You should never *indicate* that you've made a mistake.

I see people doing it all the time.

They'll make a mistake and shake their heads while smiling apologetically or say "Oh, jeez, I'm sorry" in the middle of a song, or do something that takes everyone out of the moment, including themselves.

No Director, no Casting Director, no Producer, no Music Director, no Choreographer, no Bookwriter, and no Composer wants to hear those two words or see some action that speaks the words "I'm sorry" from you.

Why?

There are a ton of reasons, but I'm going to focus on one of the major reasons I've discovered:

When you start playing the "I'm Sorry" game in the audition room, you immediately cast yourself as a *victim* in the minds of the people on the other side of the table. You're making the job of casting even harder for the creative team...the very same people that are desperately hoping that you'll be "the one" so they can stop searching and get on with making their project with *you* in it.

Let's break down the statement above.

First, the victim aspect. When you become the victim in the room, the people on the other side of the table, whether they realize it or not, have to then become your *caretakers*, they have to become your heroes. You make a mistake, then apologize, beat yourself up and become a victim of your own circumstances...then, because they're good people (most of them anyway) the people on the other side of the table then feel compelled to spend time and energy telling you everything is going to be OK, and they inevitably feel like they have to rescue you from drowning in your own despair.

An audition is kind of like a first date...in this case a date between you and the casting director/ creative team *that wants and needs to fall "in love" with you.* So, <u>let them fall in love with you</u>...warts and all!!

How many relationships have you been in where it starts out great, but as you really get to know the person, you begin to see that they are in deep need of guidance in some part of their life...and you, out of care or love, take on the role of protector or caretaker? It feels good at first, and you really do help them...but over time it becomes exhausting doesn't it?

That person doesn't change and grow, and as they stay stuck, you keep working harder and harder to save them...then, before you know it you begin to resent the very person you love and care for...you make excuses not to hang out, and there is an unspoken rift between the two of you, and it just gets bigger and bigger until the relationship ends.

I've been on both sides of that equation, and it's exhausting either way you look at it.

How many relationships like that actually end well?

Exactly!

The example "relationship" I just spoke about that in real life may last months, years, or decades... lasts a matter of minutes in the warp speed of the audition room. Don't go there!

~

Stay centered in your own power and own every mistake by pushing through and working out the problem on your own in the moment. Be your own hero, and even though you mess up, you don't need to tell anyone.

If it's a complete train wreck, let the people on the other side of table stop you--they're not evil, and they'll help you--but it will be THEM stopping you, not YOU stopping you.

~

Second, don't make it even harder on the casting people. When you make a mistake, they already know you made a mistake. They've seen and heard the same music and scenes a hundred times from the other actors that came in before you...but unlike the other actors that made a mistake and sheepishly pointed to themselves, you can push through the mistake and find your way back to the path and own your own power.

Contrary to what you might think, the people on the other side of the table won't think you're a doofus, or a bad actor, or a (fill-in-the-blank) person...they'll *respect* you.

When you can make a minor or major mistake, push through by doing something the character would do or say (staying in the moment), and then find your way back...it's thrilling to watch and lets the people on the other side of the table know that they can *trust* you, and that's huge. They'll know that you can fight through a problem on stage without falling apart...a great skill to have. It might not get you the job, but it's a huge win for you because Casting Directors love to call actors that they trust back into the room for other opportunities.

When you play the "I'm sorry" game on stage, you completely take yourself and everyone who's watching you, out of the moment.

~

It's kind of like you're a tour guide in a famous museum, and you're taking a small group of people around to different exhibits, showing them beautiful art and giving them perspectives and information they couldn't have possibly gotten on their own; they love the experience because you're literally guiding them through a finer appreciation of the artwork. Then, just as you get to the best part of the tour, a beautiful stained-glass window, you trip over some words in your prepared speech, maybe forget one or two of them. Instead of taking a well-earned moment to gather yourself...you take a crowbar out of your pocket and start smashing the glass...all the while softly saying, "I'm sorry" and shaking your head with a "what can ya do?" look on your face.

Now I know how completely ridiculous that series of events would be...but there's a lot of truth in it, and it's an example of how you can destroy a precious moment that otherwise would have been magic if you'd just followed the advice I'm giving you.

~

Listen, I am all for taking *responsibility* for your mess-ups and shortcomings in the real world, but the audition room and the stage are not the places to do that.

After the audition or performance? Yes.

During the audition? Absolutely never.

Mistakes happen.

I don't care if you have won six Tonys, been in 60 plays and musicals, and have won a lifetime achievement award or even the EGOT! Every one of those people will tell you that they have made some *huge mistakes.*

Not only have they goofed in the audition room, but also on stage in front of thousands, sometimes millions or tens of millions of people.

I'm living proof that a performer can make a gigantic mistake in front of tens of millions of people, and that pretty much all of those people can completely miss it...*if you don't let them know that you completely shit the bed!*

~

On the very first season of American Idol it was "Jazz Night" and during that week's performance, we had an awesome 16-piece Big Band behind us. It was the very first time during the run of the show that we performed with live music. Back then, everything was done to tracks, and when it was your turn to go out and sing, they just hit "play" and the music started.

Yep...the literal embodiment of the phrase, "You're on, kid!"...and Lord help you if you ever got lost with the backing tracks because there was no pause or do-overs. Each week we only had 90 seconds to sing and make our case to the millions of people watching and voting.

So, all week, leading up to the live show, we rehearsed with the band. Tensions were high, schedules were tight, and all of us (including the producers) were in uncharted waters. We knew the whole shebang could only go one of two ways...success or disaster. After all, we were the number one show in the country, and at that height, there is no middle ground.

Unfortunately, all kinds of things besides music were on my mind.

Even now, the days between live performances on Idol are filled with a mishmash of "to-do's" longer than your arm...and that's not counting rehearsals and dress rehearsals. The big "to-do" on my plate that week was solving a big debate about my costume that week.

My. Costume.

The silly debate went on all week and didn't actually get resolved until 30 seconds before I walked out on stage. What was the big deal, you ask?

My *bow tie.*

Yes folks, that's right...my bow tie. I was wearing a tux, as one does on "Jazz Night," and the million dollar question (literally) was whether my bow tie should be tied or should be loose, whether I should be casual or little swanky.

As the crowd roared steps away from the wing I was standing in, as 30 million people were tuning in to see the big show, and seconds before I had to go out and literally face the music...this was the thing the saints in wardrobe and I were thinking about.

We weren't focused on the fact that millions of dollars and ratings gold were on the line for me, the show and the network, or the fact that I was performing with a live band during one of the most important competitions of my life.

No, no, no, it was whether to tie my bow tie or leave it loose like some of the ole' time jazz singers did.

With seconds to spare I said, "Ok, ok, ok...let's just untie it and leave it loose," and wardrobe dutifully swankified me up before the stage manager shoved me (lovingly) out on to the stage.

As I made my way to zero, the band started the intro, the audience roared, the cameras got into position and the big red light on the center camera blazed into life. Knowing that there were tens of millions of people on the other side of the lens watching, I looked right into the camera and began singing.

The band was *cooking!!*

It felt so good to hear live musicians playing just feet away from me. The air was vibrating, and I felt like I was weaving my way through the most beautiful tapestry of sound and joy and love and life.

I *nailed* the first verse, I *nailed* the second verse, I *nailed* the chorus and then came the bridge...

The song?

Route 66, a very popular and well-known jazz standard. The iconic bridge of the song, written by Bobby Troup in 1946, goes like this:

"Now you go through Saint Looey
Joplin, Missouri
And Oklahoma City is mighty pretty
You see Amarillo
Gallup, New Mexico
Flagstaff, Arizona
Don't forget Winona, Kingman, Barstow, San Bernandino..." (...and so on)

But instead of singing "Flagstaff, Arizona" I sang, "Flagstaff, *Alabama.*"

I don't know why...it just came out that way. The band was blazing, everything was moving so fast and I hear myself sing, *"Alabama."*

There were two problems with this scenario:

1. *The minor problem:* The real life Route 66 highway doesn't come within almost 400 miles of any part of Alabama. I may have angered a few touchy geographers and high-minded highway enthusiasts...but all-in-all, not a career-ending move.

2. *The MAJOR problem:* "Alabama" in no way, shape, or form rhymes with "Winona" (the next word in the rhyme scheme). This was bad. Not nuclear disaster in the middle of taking a shower bad, but thanks for playing/flame's out, you're off the island/give me back the rose/Ellen hits the big red button BAD.

So, within the space of a second, I had to figure out what, if anything, rhymed with Alabama?

Internally: I was running around the stage screaming while my Afro was on fire!

Externally: I made sure to keep my cool. I just let go, and let God...

In a stroke of luck...maybe fate...it just so happens I was born in Georgia, and one of my favorite places in the world is Savannah, Georgia. It's where they shot Forrest Gump, and it is a beautiful, idyllic place with beautiful landscapes and hospitable Southerners. If you ever have or want to make up an excuse...go there, it's fab. And, in that insane moment on stage, thank goodness it came to my mind that "Alabama" rhymes with "Savannah." And, just like that, I sang:

"Flagstaff, Alabama
Don't forget Savannah
King---, Bar---, San Bernandino..."

I omitted the last halves of Kingman and Barstow (when I went back and listened to the recording, I definitely didn't say those words fully). I'm going to guess that it was due to the exhaustion from the spiritual and mental equivalent of bowel-liquefying fear.

~

The point of this story?
I managed to get away with the musical equivalent of first-degree murder because I

OWNED MY MISTAKE and instead of breaking or apologizing I relied on my wits to get me out of the problem.

Like so many performers before me, I rolled with the punches and I managed to find my way out of a problem, that in a second or so, if I had stopped and said, "I'm sorry!" or made some sort of face or judged myself or...whatever...done something that indicated that I had made a boo-boo, then the game would have been up. I might not have made it to the finals and then gone on to have a great career that's still thriving and taking me places I never even imagined I could go.

Today, I can look back at that moment and think, "Wow! That 22-year-old could've made a very different choice, and right now I could be in a very different place...and one that's not nearly as nice." I have the perspective, and distance from the event to see how one misstep could have completely changed my life.

~

Can you think back on some crazy event in your life where you "made it out alive" on stage or during a performance by the skin of your teeth...either with luck, or wits, or more likely a combination of both?

We want to hear your story!

Join The Audition Secrets Facebook Group and find out how you can see the video of my Route 66 performance and relive the story you just read in real time!

~

The audition room is the one place I give you full permission to be completely and selfishly unapologetic. I don't know if you need my permission, but I'm going to give it to you anyway.

There...now you have it.

Doesn't that feel better?

I know there's a part of you that wants to make sure that the people you're auditioning for know that you made a silly mistake.

I know you want *them* to *know* that you know you made a mistake and for them to know that you can do better... *but it's completely unnecessary.*

Showing them your mistake is doing the opposite of what you intend it to do.

It is far more powerful to make a huge mistake in front of your auditors, keep going as though nothing happened, and find your way back to the words of the scene or song, than it is to stop and start over again.

Why?

It shows the people you're auditioning for that if a mistake happens (Lord knows they always do!) that the performer in front of them can roll with it, will not fall apart on stage when something "off" happens, is trustworthy...and is a PRO!

Pros know how to make the hard stuff look easy and the easy stuff look hard.

...and guess what?

If you make that huge mistake and you plow through it, finding your way back to yourself and the scene, you're probably going to get a chance to do it all over again and get it right anyway!

That messed up first time will have not been a complete loss. If you work though the problem using the skills and creativity you've studied so hard to whip out at a moment's notice...you will have shown your auditors something special. Something that helps to get them even more on your side.

I'll tell you one more powerful story about mistakes in front of an audience...

~

Brent Carver is a Tony award-winning actor, a phenomenal person, and someone I have had the great pleasure of getting to work with. In my fourth Broadway show, I had the opportunity to play "Paris" in the play *Romeo and Juliet.*

"R & J" is my favorite literary work and a wondrous play that has been the framework for countless other stories including classics like *West Side Story.*

One night, Brent was on stage playing "Friar Laurence", a pivotal character in the play. In our show, "Romeo" was played by none other than the international superstar, Orlando Bloom. During one of their scenes together, "Friar Laurence" is speaking to "Romeo" and giving him some advice. In the middle of one of his speeches to "Romeo", Brent completely forgot what "Friar Laurence" was supposed to say...in front of a sold-out house with an international superstar patiently standing next to him on the stage.

We affectionately call completely getting lost on stage "Going into the White Room" because it feels like you've entered a white room where up / down / left / right / forward and backwards have absolutely no meaning. You're just lost.

If you've ever been in a show, and it's been running for a while, you usually get into a rhythm backstage, right?

You get used to walking past the same people at the same time and hearing the same words over the speaker at the same times. You get used to visiting certain people at certain points in the show, having conversations at a break in your track, and you know when to listen for the cues that tell you when it's time to get into position to make an entrance.

But there is this thing that happens, almost like a little invisible tap on the shoulder, when you're backstage, and something goes wrong onstage. You can be in the middle of talking with a cast mate about the most engaging topic and all of a sudden, your ears prick up because you've heard something that's not quite right...or worse...you don't hear anything at all. Where there should be music or speech, you hear dead air.

It's a weird phenomenon, and I don't know how to explain it, other than it's like a being a dog that's heard a really frightening whistle that no one else can hear.

Whenever I'm backstage during an onstage error event and I know that one of my cast mates, one of my teammates, is struggling; I automatically do "the clench" (yes, that clench, back there) and wait with bated breath to see what the outcome will be.

And this time was no different. I was terrified for Brent. Because, unlike shows that use the type of language we have been using for the past 100 years or so, the kind where you can fudge your way around the plot if you forget the exact words, this was the speech of Shakespeare's time, Old English.

When you mess up Old English...it's game over.

There is no easy way to - "I-thus-thou-dooly-whenst-thou-mayest-forgiveth-mine-self" - get out of a jam in The Bard's tongue.

We return to Brent...on Broadway, the pinnacle of the American Stage, playing one of the most well-known and loved characters in all of literary history, standing beside an international, heart-throbby superstar...and he has nowhere to go. He's lost in the desert and knows in his heart that he's out of water and that no one is coming to rescue him.

So, he does the only thing he can think to do and that's start at the beginning of the speech again to see if maybe it'll jog his memory.

We were all backstage listening, fully clenched, and all I could hear in my head was a high-pitched version of my own voice saying, "Eeeeeeeeeeeeeeeeeeeeeeeeeeeeee!"

Brent starts the speech again and it sounds strong and we're all praying he finds his way home...and then he gets to the same place he messed up before...and messes up AGAIN!

[Sidebar... If you're ever in a scene with someone and this happens to them, it always pays to know vaguely what it is that your scene partner(s)need to say. If you take this little piece of advice, you can help them out of a jam and they will love you for it. Trust me, I've helped and been helped by my scene partners more times than I can count.]

So, as I was saying, he gets to the scene's "bear-trap" and steps right into it AGAIN...then tries to back up, get a running start and fails AGAIN. I'm sweating at this point, and that's when I hear this brilliant, kind, lovely Tony-winner, in front of a full house, and standing next to the aforementioned lady-killer superstar, while performing one of the most iconic characters in all literary history, finally accept that he's come undone. He stammers a bit, and...

What does he do?

He turns to the audience and says sweetly, in a meek voice...

"Yikes!"

The audience went crazy!

They cheered and laughed because they were living the waking nightmare with him, second by second, wrapped in the thrilling terror of the moment. Only AFTER he did all that he could, retracing his steps multiple times, did he turn and own up to the mistake.

In an audition room, because there's a time element as well as a controllable pain tolerance threshold, your auditors will (99.9 times out of 100) stop you. In the real world, on the stage, the audience and perhaps even your brothers and sisters in arms in the scene with you will let you hang out to dry until you crumble to dust...if you let them.

When Brent turned to the audience and plaintively waved the white flag, the audience was just as relieved as he was when it was over, as relieved as we all were backstage as well.

Eventually, the stage manager came out, gave him the line and he was able to get through the rest of the scene and show flawlessly, all while continuing to be the wonderful person and performer that he is.

~

In Summary:

Remember, in the audition room you should never ever say, "I'm sorry," or indicate that you've made a mistake. I don't care if you completely forget everything and your hair lights on fire. Stay in the moment and do something the character would do. And while you're racking your brain trying to figure out where you are and where you're going, be like "Dory" from Disney's "Finding Nemo" and just keep swimming.

The people on the other side of the table may stop you and that's okay, but it will *not be you* stopping you. Then you can say to them, "I didn't want to stop, I wanted to keep going no matter what!" and at the very least they can respect your efforts to keep the scene alive.

The same rule applies during a performance on stage. When you get stuck, don't you dare give up the game. Keep going and roll with it. If you're in a company of people who are like-minded, you'll help each other out of the "White Room." It will be exciting and thrilling for you and the audience, and it will ultimately make you feel more connected to the moment and the work.

Rolling across the hot coals of your own error, naked, will hurt...but if you learn to take the heat, it will give you more trust in yourself and give you the experience that you need to fight through the absolute terror that those moments can cause.

~

Have you ever messed up royally in an audition or performance?

If so, what happened? How did it make you feel and what did you do? Did you learn anything from the experience?

If you want to go deeper into what it means to own your mistakes and hear about how other performers like you have overcome crazy odds to win the day, join The Audition Secrets Facebook Group.

www.facebook.com/groups/auditionsecretsvip/

I hope to see you there soon!

CHAPTER 2:
DON'T EVER LIE

For every good reason there is to tell a lie,
There is a reason to tell the truth.

- Bo Bennett

~

A single lie destroys a whole reputation
of integrity.

- Baltasar Gracian

You control the audition.

...and the audition starts the second you receive the material in your inbox.

We talk more about the whole process inside the Audition Secrets Facebook group, but for now let's talk about the part of the audition where you walk into the audition room.

When I first started auditioning, for Musical Theater in particular, I had a routine that was pretty much the same as everyone else's.

I would be at home, living with the audition material like it was a lover. Talking with it, working on making my relationship with it stronger, memorizing its lines and discovering its subtle clues, getting the feel of it into my body and becoming comfortable with it...as comfortable as anyone can be with something so new.

Like you, I would practice, practice, practice until I felt good about the material, and then make my way to the casting office on the audition day.

...and this was where things would start to go wrong.

~

I'll never forget the feelings and how they affected my mind and body.

One minute I'm walking up to the casting building and I feel excited and I'm buzzing a little, then the next minute I feel like the foolish youth in the horror movie who decided to split up from everyone else during the power outage on the same night they lost their virginity.

I begin to feel the dreaded feeling we all experience at some point or another, and that is the cold, gripping fingers of nerves!

I know exactly what's happening to me, and I can't stop it. My palms start to sweat, I get that butterflies in the stomach feeling, there's a weird tension in between my ribs and in my chest, my breathing starts to get funny, and I obsess over the places where I feel weak in the material and all the mistakes that I just can't make in the room.

You know the drill, right?

Then, to make matters worse, I walk into the casting room, and I begin to pile on the self-doubt as I look around, scoping out the competition, all the while pretending that I'm not scoping them out.

I always, ALWAYS see someone I know...and then I have to talk to them, and a part of me wants to talk to them because I adore them and don't get to see them that often...but the larger part of me just wants to sit and focus on calming down and getting the material right.

Even when I do actually get to sit down, I hear the other people going before me, the sounds of their performances wafting out from underneath the door of the audition room, and I go right ahead and judge their audition against my own choices...or lack thereof.

Finally (and yet sooner than I want) comes the dreaded moment when the Casting Assistant or the actual Casting Director calls out my name. Just when I think I'm good to go...my blood pressure, heart rate, and urge to run screaming out of the casting office spike my internal "Panic-O-Meter" into the red!"

...but on the outside, as always, I just put on my best smile, stand up, walk over to the door and into the room.

~

What a whacky experience that we all *choose* to be a part of.

Even if you're cool as a cucumber during the whole process, I have no doubt that you can tell some horror stories...we all have at least one.

Inside the Audition Secrets community, we literally spend hours talking about how to solve the many challenges we all face during the audition process, but for now, I want to focus on one specific moment.

The second you set foot in the audition room.

Here's what I used to do, and what most people still do:

- Outside of the room: panic, panic, panic (mild to severe), hear my name called, smile and do my best to shove the panic down, then walk into the room with the smile plastered to my face.

- Then, as they always do, the people who I was auditioning for would say, "Hi, how are you?" I, perhaps like you, would open my mouth and the first thing I would do upon entering the room and making my grand entrance would be...

...to LIE!

How did I lie?

I would answer their question with "Great! So great! I'm having the best day ever!" Or something to that effect, which was a blatant lie!

The feelings of panic in my heart, the "deer in the headlights look" in my eyes and the anxiety that flooded my entire body gave away the truth of how I was feeling.

And, wouldn't you know it, one of the things a Casting Director is best at is sniffing out lies and liars. People lie all day long to Casting Directors.

That lie might come from the performer in the forms of being unprepared, underprepared, or having absolutely no idea what the true meaning of what they're saying or singing is but trying to pretend that they do, or trying to make themselves look or sound impressive by bloating their resume with fictional credits...

However you try to spin it...it's a lie.

Have you ever tried to pull any of those tricks or others I didn't mention? I know I have.

I think you can guess my point: *don't ever lie.*
It doesn't matter if it's an over-airbrushed headshot, or when you're in the room and chatting.
Don't ever lie.

A good Casting Director gets a *feel* for the actor within the first 30 seconds after that actor walks in to the room.

But wait...does this mean that the Casting Director or Director or Producer will cast you or not test you based on those first 30 seconds? Absolutely not.

It varies from situation to situation, project to project, and Casting Director to Casting Director, but I know for a fact that the first impression you make is of the utmost importance for you and for the people on the other side of the table.

If the first thing you do when you walk in the room is lie, like almost everybody else does, then you have already put yourself in the big pile with all the "other actors."

Once that happens you must fight even harder to stand out.

So? I told you what not to do, but, unlike some of the other places that you can go to find do's and don'ts of auditioning, I'm going to give you a very powerful and very simple solution.

Tell the honest truth...with a twist.

~

"Wait. Are you crazy, Justin?! I should tell them the truth about my sweaty palms, my shortness of breath, and the fact that I feel like I may be having a mild heart attack?"

The simple answer is, "Yes!" But, do it with a twist.

~

Remember when I said, "You control the audition"? Well, here is a way you can play by the rules, and when I say play by the rules, I mean it. You can control any audition you walk into without lying, without trying to fool the people on the other side of the table and without trying to do things that will manipulate or alter the audition to tilt in your favor by using underhanded methods...NO!

We are not walking in that room to lie.

We are walking in that room to tell our truth and to show the people on the other side of the table why we deserve to be "the one."

That's it.

End. Of. Story.

You can control the first 30 seconds of your audition in a very simple way...by telling the truth about how you feel when the people on the other side of the table ask you the question:

"How are you today?"

Instead of lying and saying that you are just right as rain, you're going to be honest...and here's how.

By the way, if you are feeling truly calm and confident when you walk into the room, more power to you!! But keep the instructions below in your back pocket just in case...

Ready? Here we go!

If you are feeling nervous or shaky, and your auditors give you the ol' "How are ya?" simply respond by saying something like this:

"I'm actually feeling really nervous, and when I was walking here, I almost had a mild panic attack, but I'm really excited for this audition, I'm fully prepared, and with your feedback I'm going to give you the best I've got!"

All true statements!

You told them how you actually feel, you told them how you value their time and the opportunity to audition for them, you let them know you were on your A-game (prepared), and you told them that you are going to give them your best.

You also subtly mentioned that you want them to give you notes so that you can be even better for them.

Are you getting this?

Do you see how the subtle shift towards honesty (*with a twist*) can completely and powerfully change the whole audition process from the second it starts?

If every actor walked into an audition room and led with that kind of honest, vulnerable, joyful set-up (especially when they felt nervous)...it would create a whole new framework for Performers, Casting Directors, and Creative Teams to work in.

There wouldn't be this co-dependent mess of a Victim/Savior relationship going on in the room.

More importantly, we the performers, the Warrior Artists, would TAKE OUR POWER BACK.

Also, how much happier would a lot of people on the other side of the table be to not have to deal with yet another lying performer who in some way or another falls apart in the room and has to be rescued?

Here it is again, broken down into a very simple three-step process:

1. Tell them the emotions you're feeling, in as few words as possible. Just tell them how you're feeling in that moment. (Don't drag on and tell them about your Uncle Remus's pet Lemur having throat cancer, and that you couldn't find your lucky underwear, etc.)

2. Tell them how you feel about having a chance to audition for this role, and/or briefly how much you love the character or something that brings them into the present moment's joy and/or your excitement about it.

3. Let them know that you are fully prepared, you're going to give them the best you've got, and that you can't wait to hear their thoughts about your performance. You want them to give you notes, and you want to show them that you're flexible and coachable, because it ultimately makes your performance better and shows more of your range and abilities to the people on the other side of the table.

~

Note: The third step is the most important step to get right. If you say that you are fully prepared...YOU MUST BE FULLY PREPARED, or else you're dead in the water. Nothing bothers the people on the other side of the table more than a performer who's unprepared.

Being unprepared or under prepared is a waste of everyone's time and it's effectively a nail in the coffin of you not being asked back to audition for that Casting Director again.

~

In Summary:

Three steps. It's truly that simple.

When you set yourself up to not lie, it gives you ownership of your process, your truth, and your right to be a human being, not just some performance machine that has to be perfect.

Instead of giving it away the second you step into the room...you take your power back, and you can use it to shine!

Moreover, setting yourself up this way is like a breath of fresh air for the people who have to sit on the other side of the table and listen to the same old lies, and the same performances again and again for up to eight hours or more.

Don't ever lie.

You don't need to, and it's a losing game.

~

Join our outstanding community of performers and share your story about your most terrifying audition experience. We would love to hear what happened!

Did you lie?

If so, you're not alone...we all have! Join our Audition Secrets Facebook group and tell us your lies!

I hope to see you there soon!

www.facebook.com/groups/auditionsecretsvip/

CHAPTER 3:
BE AN ACTIVE LISTENER

*Most people do not listen with the
intent to understand;
they listen with the intent to reply.*

- Steven R. Covey

~

*Listening is a magnetic and strange thing, a
creative force. The friends who listen to us are the
ones we move toward. When we are listened to, it
creates us, makes us unfold and expand.*

- Karl A. Menninger

"DUHHHHH! I know that I should listen, Justin...it's in the first chapter of every book on acting.

Let me clarify.

I don't want you to just listen; I want you to be an <u>ACTIVE</u> listener.

Active Listening is one of the easiest things to do, yet one of the most challenging things to re-create in the theater unless you have a laser-like focus, or know one powerful technique...

One of the greatest listeners I've ever worked with is the inimitable Patti LuPone.

She is a lover of the words, their meaning, and even right down to the syllables of the language in the script. Patti played my mother in my first Broadway show, *Women On The Verge of a Nervous Breakdown*.

Someday, I'll tell you how crazy the experience of being thrown into the deep end with titans of the industry for my very first Broadway show was...

For now, I'll tell you one of the amazing things that happened to me onstage with Patti that let me know how amazing she was (and still is) at listening.

~

I was onstage at the Belasco Theater, in *Women On The Verge Of A Nervous Breakdown,* in the middle of a scene with Patti. We were about halfway through previews.

As you may know, the preview process is where the audience gets to see the musical or show as it's evolving, getting tighter and the actors are getting a better understanding of and experience with the material.

Because the process is fluid, oftentimes the scripts will change, sometimes massively, overnight based on what happened onstage the night before...or based on something the creators feel needs to be different in order to be more pleasing to the audience.

As a result, we performers sometimes flat out forget lines on stage when they're changing so often.

So, in the middle of a scene with Patti LuPone – Musical Theater's "Queen of New York" – I forgot what I was supposed to say. I "went up" on my lines, as they say. Being an experienced performer and knowing where my character had to end up in the plot, I started to improvise lines in order to get to where I needed to go.

For as long as I live, I will never forget the curious (at first), then knowing, then disapproving look on Miss LuPone's face as I went galloping off the ranch into my own pasture of words.

Every syllable that came out of my mouth was a feast for her...she knew I had no clue what I was supposed to say; yet she responded in the moment with gestures, facial expressions and rapt attention to every single thing that came out of my mouth.

Patti was a master "Active Listener" at work, and her eyes were ablaze.

It was at that point that I began to have this weird, burning feeling in my stomach.

In the middle of the scene, in front of a sold-out crowd, and standing next to a Goddess...I came to the full realization that I was in trouble.

Not only did Patti know my lines better than I did, but she was also unafraid (and well within her rights) to let me know on stage, in front of said sold-out crowd, that she knew I knew that what I was doing was a no-no.

...and (by silent decree, and whatever magic she used to make my stomach acid churn), that it would not, could not happen again.

Patti's really a very lovely lady. She was, and still is, so sweet and kind to me, and I learned so much from her during my first Broadway experience. She'll always be my Musical Theater Mama...

...but I won't ever mess with her like that again!

~

So, how does this delightful tale of my public embarrassment at the hands of a Theater Goddess apply to you? Well, let me tell you!

ACTIVE listening is one of the keys to success in this business.

Active Listening is kind of like watching the TV with the closed captioning on, but in real life, not just on the screen.

Here's the cool part: when you get good at it, it will feel kind of like you're reading a cartoon where the words come out of people's mouths in thought bubbles. It sounds crazy, I know! The funny thing is, that we do it all the time in real life with our family and our friends, but so many of us forget to do it while we're performing with our cast mates.

I'll give you an example: have you ever had a friend or a family member tell you a story about something super gross or scary that happened to them?

My wife has had a lot of freaky ghost experiences.

One time she was telling me about how she was sitting on the back porch of her childhood home with her best friend, just relaxing and talking. Suddenly, as though someone had cupped their hands, and gotten close to her ear...she heard a voice whisper her name: "Hey, Reina."

The hairs stood up on her neck, she screamed, and got up and swatted at her ear. As she was telling me this story I was like, "Oh my gosh NO WAY!!"

I was totally there with her... it even gave me the willies a bit. I was able to tune out everything that was happening around me, and I was hanging on every word.

Do you ever find the same thing happening to you?

If you experience this when someone tells you a story, then you are ACTIVELY Listening. We do it all the time when we listen and react to the moment-to-moment roller coaster ride of the funny or crazy stories people tell us.

It isn't any different on stage. You've heard the phrase "keep the ball in the air,"?

It's a common phrase that we use in the theater to say keep the momentum alive and keep the energy bouncing back and forth between the people speaking in the scene.

"Active Listening" is one of the keys to making that work.

In Summary:

Here's a great exercise I call "Lip Locking" to get you started.I named it that because it's a bit of a saucy title and it will stick in your brain!

"Lip Locking" is a simple 3-step process and it works best if I can demonstrate it to you, but here I'll describe it to you.

First, find a partner to work with. They don't need to be a performer, just someone with lips. Ask them to read something or give them a topic to talk about...they can say anything (it doesn't matter) at a ***normal conversational pace.***

When you say "go," have them start talking, and as they speak, look only at their lips, and speak the words you see and hear **out loud** along with them, word for word, as quickly as you can.

If you're doing it right, it will sound like there's a slight echo in the room because you'll be saying your partner's words a millisecond after they do.

Next, do the same setup, but instead of saying the words out loud with them, you're just going to silently mouth the words you hear (moving your lips but not making a sound) as you watch their mouth and listen.

Have your partner say or read something different so you don't anticipate the words they're going to say

Ok, here's the final part of the exercise: Same set up.

Watch your partner's mouth, listen and repeat the words they say...but this time don't say it out loud and don't move your lips and mouth along, just say the words in your head.

How did you do?

Did you notice how the world phased out and there was nothing going on in your mind but whatever was coming out of your partner's mouth?

If you did, then you're on your way to becoming a master at Active Listening.

Try this technique (it's fun to do with your friends and family) and see how it works in your everyday life. Once you feel comfortable with it, start trying it in the audition room and during performances.

You'll start to see that you're more in the moment and "keeping the ball in the air" with your scene partners more easily!

Do this exercise, and you'll become a laser-focused Active Listener.

~

If you'd like to find out how you can see my "Lip Locking" training video where I do the exercise with you and become your "Lip Locking" partner head on over to Facebook and join the Audition Secrets group!

There's a ton of great information and even more secrets waiting for you!

www.facebook.com/groups/auditionsecretsvip

CHAPTER 4:
THE CASTING TEAM IS ON YOUR SIDE

*We are always thinking about all our shows
— so an actor who isn't right for the particular
show might be right for something else.
Showing up that day is a good way to remind us
that you're in town and ready to work.*

- Tara Rubin, Tara Rubin Casting, NYC

~

*Actors and casting directors are team players.
Unfortunately, many actors think:
"Please, call me in to audition. You're so important
to me. Let me put you on this pedestal."
Oh my gosh, please, no!
We are equals in this game, my friends.
Don't try to impress us. Don't bow down before us.
Don't try to shake our hands. Don't be aggressive.
It's not up to the Casting Director whether you
book the job or not. That decision is up to our
clients [The Director, Producers, etc].
If you look good and do well in an audition, then I
look good to my clients. Just be real. We like that.
It's just that simple.*

- Ken Lazer, Casting Director

This is a simple concept, yet so powerful.

So many of the performers that I work with, and even more of the performers who are my peers, have stories about how they walked into a casting room and felt like the Casting Director and the creative team hated them.

They actually felt as if the Casting Director legitimately disliked them as a person, which sounds absurd to non-performers, but every single one of us who has ever walked into an audition knows and understands the feeling, right?

When we take a moment to create a bit of a shift in our thinking and look at things from the Casting Director's point of view, we see a whole different story.

Good Casting Directors are like diamonds; they come in all shapes and sizes, and they're all valuable. Like diamonds, the best Casting Directors are formed under immense pressure. There is a huge amount of pressure put on Casting Directors every single day.

They must to be able to consistently spread their nets wide and bring in not just any actor, but actors who are actually right for the roles that are being cast...but how do they know the actors that are actually right for the roles? It's an art that is as much logic as it is intuition.

Not only that, but when choosing actors, they also must make sure that they are getting a diverse and rich palette of colors, ethnicities and looks so that the creative team feel like a group of kids in a candy store with the week's allowance in their pockets.

If Casting Directors don't have a large stable of good actors to call on and can't manage to find "the one" or "ones" on a consistent basis...they aren't going to be Casting Directors for very long.

One of the greatest things you can remember when you walk into the audition room: the Casting Director is hoping and praying (*sometimes desperately*) that you'll be "the one."

They want you to succeed, and sometimes they even need you to succeed and have the most awesome audition ever!!

Does that make sense?

They want to find their Star so the pressure can be off of them. Just as performers love the challenge of getting up on stage and delivering a great performance...a lot of Casting Directors really love and live for the challenge of finding that perfect person.

> *If you haven't joined yet our Audition Secrets Facebook Group, you're missing out on being part of a diverse and awesome community of people who are on the hunt for consistent success, just like you.*
>
> *Stay on point!*
>
> *www.facebook.com/groups/auditionsecretsvip/ to learn more and to join.*

The casting process is like a huge game of "Where's Waldo?" for Casting Directors.

Remember, like diamonds, they are under a tremendous amount of pressure on their end of the game, just like we are on our end.

The Casting Team is ALWAYS on your side, and they want you to have the best audition performance ever!

~

CHAPTER 5:
THIS IS SUPPOSED
TO BE FUN

One of the fun parts about becoming an actor:
You can become whoever you want to be.

- Michael B. Jordan

~

It's so funny, you go to acting school thinking that
you're going to learn to be other people, but really,
it taught me how to be myself.
Because it's in understanding yourself deeply that
you can lend yourself deeply to another person's
circumstances and another person's experience.

- Lupita Nyong'o

I saved this one for last because it's probably the most important secret to remember, and all of us, no matter what level we're at, can easily forget this simple principal.

This is supposed to be fun.

In fact, playwright Noël Coward wrote, "Work is much more fun than fun."

Wouldn't it be great if we could live up to that with our artistic work?

When we are in the middle of preparing for auditions or performances or whatever, it's easy to lose sight of the reasons why we got into this game.

Take a moment to think about your reasons why.

One of mine: I live to perform. Getting in front of a huge crowd and entertaining and educating them is like cat-nip for me, and I get to give and receive massive amounts of energy, love, and LIFE in the process. It just feels right...and it feels natural, although like you, I've worked hard to make it feel natural!

One of the greatest shifts I've made in my career was learning how to make the audition and performance process *fun*. No matter the outcome.

By taking the concepts in this book (as well as others we talk about in the Audition Secrets universe) and applying them to my performance life, I've opened myself up. I've helped myself to just relax as I go into the audition room or step on the stage, and so have so many other performers I've worked with.

I choose to be my authentic self and own the good, the bad, the ugly, the indifferent, the amazing, the mediocre, and everything else in between that happens when I'm in the room or on the stage.

I choose to stand tall, strong, and grounded in **my power**. Grounded in the truth of who I am. Take it or leave it.

If you can go into the audition and performance process like that, you will immediately begin to create a reputation for yourself as someone who the people on the other side of the table are excited to see.

You, of course, <u>must do good work</u>. It's not just a "fun fest" in the audition room/stage where you're testing out some new jokes...there is serious work to be done.

You also must own your *own* power...not try to reduce or vampire other people's power by lording over them, or "showing" your power by being cocky or overconfident.

Just be your best self. Live your best life!

It's so much better to perform in the room and on the stage under the umbrella of joy and excitement and fun. Believe me, the people in the room who see 99.9 percent of the actors coming in being nervous, unhappy to be there, or ready to run out of the room screaming, will thank you for being the 0.1 percent that comes in prepared, honest, confident and ready to do the work!

I tell my students all the time, when they start to freak out and beat up on themselves because they're struggling in one place or another:

"Remember, this is supposed to be fun.
Our job is to play! While most people get dressed up to go sit at a desk...our job is to get dressed up and play!"

Yet most times, we manage to make it so serious and so crushing that it no longer is something that brings us joy.

If you're feeling like this business is a 10-ton elephant that's weighing on you, but you don't want to give up on it, then I suggest you try a very simple exercise.

Please take out a journal or open a voice notes app on your phone, and I want you to tell yourself or someone else you care about:

Your **"Origin Story."**

You know how the superhero movies have "origin stories" where the character who was a normal person, on a normal day, touched some sort of radioactive goo or got bit by some rare insect...and suddenly, their lives were completely changed?

Their bodies were changed,
Their minds were changed,
Their internal chemistry was changed...
and they became Superheroes.

Well...that moment when you were inspired to become a performer is your version of the Superhero "origin story.

Write it down, speak it out, and in so doing you can get back in touch with the reason why you started this crazy journey in the first place, and it just might give you the spark of inspiration...the spark of courage that you need to keep going that extra inch, that "one more audition."

~

There is a very famous story about a man who went out to California during the gold rush days, and like other prospectors looking for their fortune, he staked his claim and began digging for gold.

He had some success but wanted to dig deeper and try and find what is called the "Mother Lode", a main-vein and massive amount of gold...but he wasn't able find it...so he kept digging and digging, and he kept spending more and more money.

Finally, he got to the point where he felt he had to give up because if he didn't, he would go completely broke. After digging for months and months finding success here and there, he ended up never finding what he was truly looking for.

So, he sold his claim, which was worthless to him, for pennies on the dollar to the first person that came along. He gave up and he went back East.

The next person who came along hired another person who was an expert in the study of the rocks and minerals in the area...and working side by side, they discovered that all they needed to do was dig three more inches in the right direction and they would hit a Mother Lode of Gold.

In the very same dusty patch that the old prospector thought was worthless and sold off for pennies, there was the opportunity for another person to become wealthy.

The two new claim owners dug three more inches, and not only did they hit the Mother Lode, but their claim became one of the biggest and most profitable gold mines in the history of the Gold Rush.

All because he just kept going a few more inches where someone else had given up.

~

Telling your "Origin Story" can be to you like digging a few more inches was to them.

Science has shown that the people who are ultra-successful in life and business aren't successful because they're smarter or more talented...but because they put in just a bit more effort than everyone else. They're willing to go that 1 extra mile, more often, and they end up getting miles ahead of the competition as a result.

That's it...so can you put in just that little bit extra to propel yourself ahead of the rest, and out from the stampeding herd?

Am I making sense?

What is your origin story?

How can you dig a few inches deeper to find the Mother Lode of joy and fun that is unique only to you?

Because, if you can get there, it will give you the strength and the courage to dig a few more inches and to go to a few more auditions, to work on your skills just that little bit more than your peers so that you can achieve your dreams and achieve them faster. You are allowed to be having a good time. Our job is one of the greatest jobs in the world because we get paid to play.

This is supposed to be fun!!

~

Can you see why it might be a good idea to join us in the Audition Secrets Facebook membership group?

We're here to support you on your journey, wherever it takes you!

Join now!

www.facebook.com/groups/auditionsecretsvip/

LET'S RISE TOGETHER

When you go in the audition room or step out on to the stage, do the things that I've shown you in this book, and apply the powerful secrets and techniques found in the **Audition Secrets** community, you can and will own every audition room you walk into and every stage you walk onto.

In the audition room, you might not get the job on the first try, but you will make the people who hold the keys to the kind of success you want stand up and start to notice you like they never have before... if you walk the path with me and the other Warrior Artists in our community.

When you can own every audition or performance every single time and you can dissect and learn from each experience you have in the room or on the stage, you can and will feel good about yourself and finally feel confident about your efforts on a *consistent* basis.

It may seem like we need to go into the audition room and give the Casting Team exactly what it is that they're "looking for." But that's the exact opposite of what I'm encouraging you to do.

I want you to give them YOU! Be willing to be yourself...you might not realize it now, but it's the very best part of you!

When you step into the room or on the stage and begin to truly live the concept of completely owning who you are and how you feel in the moment, you'll learn that there is no one in the world like you and no one in the world who can deliver your unique performance.

Then, when you truly understand the simple and powerful mindsets and skill sets that are waiting to be discovered inside the **Audition Secrets Community,** you'll begin creating the kinds of performances that can bring you closer and closer to your goal of booking more and better jobs!

You and I have spent so much time and money working hard to not only learn but to *live* the techniques and skills it takes to be a performer. We go to school, to the acting studio, the dance studio, we get coached, we work hard to find and maintain an agent, and we pound the pavement every day working toward our goals.

But in school, no one taught you the secrets of auditioning, no one taught you the proven methods of how to own a room. No one taught you the cutting edge and vital skills that can set you apart from the millions of other actors out there.

What you'll find in this book is just the first step in your journey to truly becoming a **Warrior Artist.**

This is the beginning of a new way to approach your art and performances that will not only help you nail auditions and performances and book more jobs but take you on a journey that will teach you more about yourself and finally reveal the secrets and skill sets you need to make your mark on this business.

I am inviting you, with open arms, into a community of passionate, powerful, and purpose-driven artists you can learn from, grow with, and join hands with to create an alliance so that we can all RISE TOGETHER and have the clarity, focus, and power to achieve our own unique versions of success.

That is the promise that we in the Audition Secrets community make to you.

The only thing we require is that you play full out.

There are no guarantees in this business, you know that or you wouldn't have bothered to be in this business...but the one thing that we can guarantee is that if you play full out, learn and live the concepts and skill sets I set before you in this book and in The Audition Secrets community,

YOU WILL GROW,

YOU WILL GET BETTER,

YOU WILL OWN THE ROOM & STAGE,

and you will exponentially increase your chances of booking more and better jobs.

The next move is yours.

www.facebook.com/groups/auditionsecretsvip/

MEET JUSTIN

Justin Bell Guarini's robust professional performance career launched with the first season of American Idol in 2002. His stage and screen appearances since then include principal roles in six Broadway productions (most notably *American Idiot, Romeo and Juliet, Wicked,* and *In Transit*) as well as hosting in-studio shows for The TV Guide Network along with hosting live red-carpet events, the Oscars, the Emmys, and the Grammys. He continues to reprise his role as the lovable Lil' Sweet in nationally televised commercials for Diet Dr. Pepper.

Justin has advocated for music education funding on Capitol Hill by lobbying for the International Music Products Association. He has worked with Education Through Music Los Angeles, a nonprofit  utilizing music education as a catalyst to improve academic achievement, motivation for school, and self-confidence in underserved communities. Justin has also partnered with RandomActs.org and

GISH.com to participate in global kindness campaigns.

In 2019, Justin founded The Warrior Artist Alliance to help performers achieve success in a challenging industry. He shares his tips, tricks, breadth of experience, and warrior mindset with a community of performers through podcasts, blogs, and dynamic training programs.

Justin is dedicated to his loving family. His wife, daughter and sons make up his happy home. It is here that he draws his support and the desire to live his best life.

Learn more at www.JustinGuarini.com.

54436247R00073

Made in the USA
San Bernardino,
CA